Practical Know-how in the Kitchen

SIMON &
SCHUSTER

LONDON • NEW YORK • SYDNEY • TORONTO

First published in Great Britain by
Simon & Schuster UK Ltd 2007
A CBS Company

ISBN 1 8473 70063

Simon and Schuster UK Ltd
Africa House
64–78 Kingsway
London WC2B 6AH

1 3 5 7 9 10 8 6 4 2

Design and illustrations by Jane Norman
Jacket design by Kari Brownlie
Printed and bound in China

Contents

Introduction

How can you stop boiled eggs from cracking, revive stale bread, weigh treacle and freeze leftover cream? What's the secret of a perfect roast or a feather-light sponge cake, and how do you cook Christmas dinner without having a nervous breakdown?

Unless you're a budding domestic goddess, you need good, practical advice, and where better to find it than from the Women's Institute, whose members are famed for their culinary expertise. As well as offering pearls of wisdom, this little book contains entertaining quotations about food that span the centuries from ancient Greece to the 21st century.

" *There is no sincerer love than the love of food.* **"**

George Bernard Shaw 1856–1950

Cook's Tips

Measuring ingredients

If you still work in imperial (pounds and ounces), note that one lightly heaped tablespoon of flour or sugar is equal to an ounce.

To check if an egg is fresh

Carefully put the egg in a bowl of cold water.

A really fresh egg will sink to the bottom.

One that floats is definitely off – throw it away.

Anything in the middle is acceptable.

❋

66 *I have met a lot of hardboiled eggs in my time, but you're twenty minutes.* **99**

Oscar Wilde, 1854–1900

To shell a hard-boiled egg

To stop the eggs from going black around the
yolk and to peel them easily: as soon as they
are cooked, drain and run under cold water. Tap
them gently to crack the shells for easy peeling.
Leave under cold running water or in several
changes of cold water for 5–6 minutes.

To stop boiled eggs cracking

Add 1 tablespoon of vinegar or 1 teaspoon of
salt to the water in which the eggs
are to be boiled.

Olive oil

Always try to buy the best olive oil you can afford. Usually the darker green the oil, the richer the flavour. The best quality supermarket own-brand is nearly always better value than the well-known brands.

Parmesan cheese

Don't waste money on ready-grated Parmesan cheese. Buy a piece of fresh Parmesan and keep it well wrapped (cling film and foil) in the fridge or freezer. When required, just unwrap and grate as much as you need.

✺

"The early bird gets the worm, but the second mouse gets the cheese."

Jon Hammond

Buying pasta

A good brand of dried pasta is far superior to most fresh pasta offered in supermarkets. The Italians mostly use dried and make their own only for special occasions. They buy fresh only from a good local producer.

" No man is lonely eating spaghetti;
it requires so much attention."

Christopher Morley, 1890–1957

" Everything you see I owe to spaghetti."

Sophia Loren b.1934

Choosing pasta shapes

Short tubular pasta (e.g. rigatoni, penne, macaroni) is best used in baked dishes with vegetables, cheese and meat.

✳

Smooth long pasta (e.g. spaghetti, linguine) is best with sauces such as Bolognese, tomato and clams as these keep the pasta slippery and separate.

✳

Cup-shaped pasta (e.g. conchiglie, orecchiette) is designed to hold sauces with larger ingredients such as mushrooms, artichokes and tomatoes.

✳

Cut pasta (e.g. tagliatelle, fettuccine) is best eaten with rich sauces made with cream, eggs or meat.

✳

Twisted pasta (e.g. fusilli, farfalle). The curly character of these pastas means that they will trap thin sauces such as pesto, garlic, and olive oil flavoured with chilli.

✳

Tiny pasta shapes (e.g. alphabet letters, fillini, vermicelli) cook quickly and are ideal for adding to soups and casseroles.

Keep herbs handy

Some fresh herbs freeze well: chopped parsley can be frozen then added to sauces and other hot dishes. All the thymes, rosemary and sage freeze well. Freeze on their stalks and rub or shake to remove the leaves. Herbs with softer leaves, such as tarragon and basil, do not freeze well, neither do bay leaves.

Best basil

Fresh basil can either be grown as a plant or bought in small bunches. It looses its flavour when cooked, so be sure to add it at the last moment or keep it fresh and bright. Either tear the leaves or chop them.

" *Oh, better no doubt is a dinner of herbs,*

When season'd with love,

which no rancour disturbs

And sweeten'd by all that is sweetest in life

Than turbot, bisque, ortolans,

eaten in strife! **"**

Edward Bulwer-Lytton, 1831–1891

Full-flavoured rosemary

Sit the joint on a large sprig of rosemary when roasting. This will also give the gravy a good flavour. Rosemary is good finely chopped and added to fried potatoes. When finely chopped, it can also be used in sweet biscuits.

To keep cut parsley and coriander fresh

Put in a hole-free polythene bag with a couple of tablespoons of cold water, give the bag a good shake and keep in the salad drawer of the fridge. Both herbs should keep for at least a week.

As for rosemary, I let it run all over my garden walls, not only because my bees love it but because it is the herb sacred to remembrance and to friendship, whence a sprig of it hath a dumb language.

Sir Thomas More, 1478–1535

" *If one consults enough herbals...every sickness known to humanity will be listed as being cured by sage.* **"**

Herb expert

To stop avocado turning brown

Lemon juice helps to stop cut avocados turning
brown. Also, if you pop the avocado stone into
a bowl of guacamole or salsa, this will keep the
dip fresh and green for at least 2 hours;
remove the stone before serving!

Sage fritters

For something different try sage fritters. Dip
whole leaves into a light batter (batter made
with lager is good) and deep fry in sunflower oil
until golden. Drain on kitchen paper and serve
with mayonnaise, with some chopped parsley
and lemon juice added.

To remove insects from vegetables

Fill a sink or bowl with cold water and add a couple of tablespoons of salt. Leave the vegetables or salad leaves to soak for about 20 minutes. The insects will sink to the bottom of the bowl and you can then clean the vegetables as normal.

"No clever arrangement of bad eggs ever made a good omelette."

C.S Lewis 1898–1963

For plump dried fruit

Pour boiling water over the dried fruit and leave
to stand for 30 minutes: add a tea bag for
flavour. For special occasions, leave fruit to
soak overnight in brandy or rum.

*❝ Food is our common ground,
a universal experience. ❞*

James Beard, 1903–1985

Weighing treacle or syrup

If it is to be melted, weigh the syrup in the saucepan – put the pan on the scales, put the scales back to zero and add the syrup.

*

To slide the syrup or treacle from a measuring spoon easily, dip the tablespoon into flour, shake, and then dip into the treacle.

*

Heat a tablespoon in a gas flame or in boiling water and then immediately use it to scoop out the syrup.

" I asked the waiter, 'Is this milk fresh?' He said, 'Lady, three hours ago it was grass.'**"**

Phyllis Diller, b.1917

Money Savers

To use up sour milk

If milk turns sour (and this is when it smells
or tastes sour not when it has reached the
best-before date) it is excellent
for making scones.

Sun-blush tomatoes from sun-dried

Sun-blush tomatoes are softer, juicier and more
expensive than sun-dried, so try this: pour
boiling water over the sun-dried tomatoes
and leave them for 20–30 minutes.
Drain well and use.

To revive old nuts

Bring back flavour and texture to slightly stale
flaked almonds, walnuts or hazelnuts by gently
roasting them in a dry frying pan. Be sure to
swirl and shake the pan until the nuts
become lightly brown, taking care
not to burn them.

✳

*If 'ifs' and 'buts' were candy and nuts,
wouldn't it be a Merry Christmas?*

Anon.

Freeze leftover cream

Freeze spare cream in an ice cube tray,
and then turn out the cubes into a sealed bag
for storage. The cubes are useful for enriching
soups and sauces. Add frozen to hot
liquid and heat gently.

❋

❝ *The friendly cow, all red and white, I love
with all my heart; She gives me cream with
all her might, To eat with apple-tart.* **❞**

Robert Louis Stevenson, 1850–1894

To get more juice from a lemon or lime

Roll the fruit on a hard surface with your hand.
Alternatively cook the fruit on high in the
microwave for just 10 seconds,
cool then squeeze.

*

" *When fate hands you a lemon,
make lemonade.* "

Dale Carnegie, 1888–1955

To crisp up a day-old crusty loaf

Hold the loaf very briefly under a running cold tap. Give it a good shake and pop in a hot oven for about 10 minutes; it will be as soft and crusty as a freshly baked loaf.

To make dry breadcrumbs

Don't waste money on bought breadcrumbs.
Dry slices of white or wholemeal bread on a
baking sheet in the oven (just pop them in
when something else is cooking or has just
finished cooking). When they are cold, whiz in a
food processor or blender and store in a
polythene bag in the freezer.

❋

❝*If you have two loaves of bread,
sell one and buy a lily.***❞**

Chinese proverb

A perfectly ripe avocado

Buy avocados hard as they are always cheaper.
Ripen on your window-sill or put them in a
paper bag (or a dark drawer) with a banana.
Ethylene gas is used commercially to ripen
bananas and the residue will help the avocado
or other fruit to ripen quickly. A ripe avocado
should feel like butter at room temperature,
when squeezed.

Will it freeze?

Egg whites and yolks can be frozen separately.
Label how many there are in each container.
Leave egg whites to thaw naturally. They are
good for making meringues. Yolks will
keep for 4–5 weeks.

❋

❝ *Love and eggs are best when*
they are fresh. **❞**

Russian proverb.

Too many tomatoes

Tomatoes can be frozen whole in polythene bags. They can then be used in place of canned tomatoes in sauces: just add whole frozen tomatoes to the pan when you would normally add the canned tomatoes.

❝ *A world devoid of tomato soup, tomato sauce, tomato ketchup and tomato paste is hard to visualize...How did the Italians eat spaghetti before the advent of the tomato? Was there such a thing as tomato-less Neapolitan pizza?* **❞**

Elizabeth David, 1913–1992

" *Why do croûtons come in airtight packages? It's just stale bread to begin with.* **"**

George Carlin, b.1937

Appliances that Help

Make the most of your food processor

Keep your food processor on the work surface not in a cupboard; if it's ready to go you'll use it more often. You can buy a cover for it or drape a tea towel over it to keep the dust off.

Microwave meringues

Take 1 medium egg white and stir in about 325 g (11 oz) sifted icing sugar, adding enough to make a pliable mixture that you are able to roll into balls about the size of a small walnut. Put 2 balls on to a plate lined with kitchen paper. Microwave on high for 30–40 seconds, until the balls are puffed up and spread out into meringues. Watch closely as they soon turn brown. Sandwich together with cream and soft fruit.

A good steamer

Treat yourself to a Chinese bamboo steamer:
they're cheap and good for steaming
vegetables, fish and meat. You can pile one on
top of the other over a large saucepan or
wok to cook layers of food.

❋

" *Talk doesn't cook rice.* **"**

Chinese proverb

Instant crispy croûtons

Remove the crusts from white bread then
cut them into cubes. Lay in a single layer on
a plate covered with greaseproof paper
and microwave on high for
2 minutes until crisp.

Efficient grilling machine

These work-top griddles (the type promoted by
the American celebrity boxer) are really good.
They cook food quickly and healthily and the
food doesn't spit in the way that it
does on an open griddle.

Non-stick microwaved porridge for one

Put 50 g (2 oz) porridge oats in a bowl and stir in 300 ml (½ pt) milk until well mixed. Microwave on high for 4–5 minutes, stirring a couple of times. Add a pinch of salt if you like and leave to stand for 2 minutes. Serve with brown sugar, golden syrup, marmalade, honey or jam for a great start to the day.

❋

" *Spare your breath to cool your porridge.* **"**

Miguel de Cervantes, 1547–1616

To warm plates for serving

Microwave on high for 1 minute. Make sure
they don't have any metal decoration on them.

Flowers in ice cubes

Freezing edible flowers in ice cubes is good for
a summer party. Borage (a small blue flower)
looks pretty and so do individual golden
marigold petals.

> **"** *Like fragile ice*
> *anger passes away in time.* **"**

Ovid, Ancient Roman poet

" *Although I cannot lay an egg, I am a very good judge of omelettes.* **"**

George Bernard Shaw, 1856–1950

The Kitchen Novice

Omelette implements

I use a cheap non-stick pan with a metal palette knife to make omelettes: they last about a year and then I replace them. You will read a lot about seasoning special pans for omelettes, but this is the easiest way.

How to make French dressing

Put 4 tablespoons of sunflower oil (or half olive oil), 4 teaspoons of white wine, tarragon or cider vinegar, a good pinch of sugar, 1 teaspoon of French mustard (seedy if you like), 1 crushed garlic clove, salt and freshly ground black paper in a screw-top jar. Shake vigorously, taste and adjust the seasoning. This will keep in the fridge for 3–4 weeks.

Our Garrick's a salad; for in him we see, Oil, vinegar, sugar and saltiness agree.

Oliver Goldsmith, 1730–1774

66 *Dost thou think because thou art virtuous there shall be no more cakes and ale?* 99

William Shakespeare, 1564–1616

✳

66 *A compromise is the art of dividing a cake in such a way that everyone believes he has the biggest piece.* 99

Ludwig Erhard, 1897–1977

Quick sponge cake

Put 100g (4 oz) soft tub margarine, caster sugar and self-raising flour (replace 25 g/1 oz flour with cocoa for a chocolate sponge) with 2 medium eggs in a food processor (or a bowl and use an electric whisk) and whiz together for 2 minutes until well mixed. Pour into a greased and lined 15cm (6 in) cake tin. Bake for 20–25 minutes at Gas Mark 6/200°C/400°F until the surface springs back when gently touched. Leave for 5 minutes then remove from the tin and cool on a wire rack.

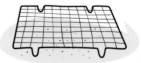

Rescuing a sponge cake

Remember that sieved icing sugar and/or
cocoa powder will cover a multitude of sins.
For fillings use jam and cream, butter cream or
try whipped cream flavoured with cocoa for a
chocolate sponge, or hazelnut spread.

*❝ You know you are getting old when the
candles cost more than the cake. ❞*

Bob Hope, 1903–2003

"The jelly – the jam and the marmalade,
And the cherry-and-quince preserves she made!
And the sweet-sour pickles of peach and pear,
With cinnamon in 'em and all things rare!
And the more we ate was the more to spare,
Out to old Aunt Mary's! Ah!"

James Whitcomb Riley, 1849–1916

Jam and
Marmalade Tips

The right sugar

Use sugar made from imported sugar cane.
British sugar is made from sugar beet and it
can be very difficult to get jam and
marmalade to set using sugar made
from sugar beet.

"*Oxford gave the world marmalade and a manner, Cambridge science and a sausage.*"

Anon.

Oranges and lemons

Seville oranges are the best for making marmalade; they are available in January and February. However, it is possible to make a good marmalade with equal quantities of lemons, grapefruit and regular sweet oranges. This is known as Three Fruit Marmalade.

Cooking the fruit

Always make sure that the fruit is completely cooked and soft before adding the sugar. Once the sugar is added the fruit will not continue to cook and soften.

❝The rule is, jam tomorrow and jam yesterday – but never jam today.**❞**

Lewis Carroll, 1832–1898

❝The Law of Raspberry Jam: the wider any culture is spread, the thinner it gets.**❞**

Alvin Toffler b. 1928

For fruit low in pectin

Some fruit, like strawberries, are low in pectin, the natural substance in fruit that helps jam to set. Add 50 g (2 oz) cranberries to each 450 g (I lb) soft fruit. Alternatively try adding lemon juice or the juice of cooked gooseberries, apples, blackcurrants or redcurrants.

To test for setting point

Chill a bone china plate in the freezer for
30 minutes. Drop a little jam or marmalade on
to the plate and push the surface with your
fingertip: it should wrinkle a little where it has
formed a skin. Alternatively, hold a sugar
thermometer in the boiling jam, without
touching the bottom of the pan, and
check the temperature.
Jam sets at about 104°C (220°F).

Scum on the surface?

If there is scum on the surface of jam ready to
pot, add a very small knob of butter and stir in
well. Leave for a few seconds before potting,
during which time the surface of the jam
will become smooth and clear.

Jars and lids

Save jars and screw lids throughout the year.
If you don't have lids, use a circle of
cellophane, parchment or greaseproof paper to
cover the surface of the jam. Secure this with
an elastic band or some string. Put the
lids or covers on immediately.

❝ *And the Quangle Wangle said To himself on the Crumpetty Tree, 'Jam; and Jelly; and bread; Are the best of food for me!* **❞**

Edward Lear, 1812–1888

❝ *Wit ought to be a glorious treat like caviar; never spread it about like marmalade.* **❞**

Noel Coward, 1899–1973

"The feeling of friendship is like that of being comfortably filled with roast beef; love, like being enlivened with champagne."

Samuel Johnson, 1709–1784

The Perfect Roast

Best beef

Boned and rolled sirloin and rib, preferably on
the bone – either fore rib, middle rib or wing rib
– are best for roasting. Topside can be roasted
but is often dry and needs some fat
around it. It is best pot-roasted.

" Oh! The roast beef of England,
And old England's roast beef. "

Henry Fielding, 1707–1754

" The road turns and the town suddenly
springs into view, presenting itself like
a crown roast of lamb served on a
bed of fresh spring greens. "

Maria Donovan

Lamb

Leg, shoulder and best end of neck, also known as rack of lamb, are best for roasting. Both shoulder and leg are sold whole or in halves. Shoulder has the sweeter, though fattier meat and is more difficult to carve. Leg is usually more expensive but less fatty and easy to carve. Breast of lamb is a very economical cut and is usually sold boned, stuffed and rolled, ready for roasting; it is fatty but good.

Pork

The cuts are loin, half legs, belly and a cut
known as the hand and spring, which is the
front shoulder. Loin (on or off the bone) is
superior as the meat is sweet and the
crackling is marvellous. If you buy a joint
on the bone, get the butcher to chine
(saw through the backbone) so that
you can carve more easily.

Perfect pork crackling

First, ask your butcher to score the pork skin.
Just before putting the pork into the oven, rub
the skin with water (not oil) and sprinkle over
table salt so that it sticks to the surface.
Occasionally the skin won't crisp; don't
blame yourself: it happens.

*

" *Kissing don't last: cookery do!* **"**

George Meredith 1828–1909

Here's a toast to the roast that good fellowship lends, With the sparkle of beer and wine; May its sentiment always be deeper, my friends, Than the foam at the top of the stein.

Anon.

Resting before eating

Do rest the meat for about 10 minutes or more after cooking and before carving. Then transfer it to a warm serving platter, cover with foil to keep the heat in and set aside. This gives you time to make the gravy and the meat time to firm up.

✳

" *Great boast, small roast* **"**

Proverb

Roasting times

Beef on the bone

Oven temperature: Gas Mark 6/200°C/400°F.
Allow 15 minutes per 450 g (1 lb), plus
15 minutes extra. For medium-rare beef, do not
cook for the extra 15 minutes.

Beef off the bone

Oven temperature Gas Mark 6/200°C/400°F.
Allow 20 minutes per 450 g (1 lb), plus
20 minutes extra. For medium-rare beef, do not
cook for the extra 20 minutes.

Lamb on the bone

Oven temperature: Gas Mark 6/200°C/400°F.
Allow 20 minutes per 450 g (1 lb) plus
20 minutes. If you like lamb slightly pink in the
middle, do not cook for the extra 20 minutes.

Lamb off the bone

Oven temperature: Gas Mark 6/200°C/400°F.
Allow 25 minutes per 450 g (1 lb) plus
20 minutes. For slightly pink lamb, leave out
the extra 25 minutes.

Pork on the bone

Oven temperature: Gas Mark 6/200°C/400°F.
Allow 25 minutes per 450 (1 lb), plus
25 minutes extra. Pork is served cooked all the
way through, never pink or rare.

Pork off the bone

Oven temperature: Gas Mark 5/190°C/375°F.
Allow per 450 (1 lb), plus 35 minutes extra.
Pork is served cooked all the way through,
never pink or rare.

To make a supermarket chicken more interesting

For an average 1.5 kg (3 lb 5 oz) bird. If it is frozen, let it defrost for 24 hours in the fridge. Cut an onion in half, keeping the skin. Place half the onion, half a lemon (squeezed) and a sprig of rosemary or thyme inside the cavity. Put the chicken and the other half an onion into the roasting tin. Rub butter or olive oil over the whole of the chicken. Sprinkle with a little salt and freshly ground black pepper. Add about 1 cm (½ inch) water to the roasting tin and cover with foil. Roast the chicken at Gas Mark 6/200°C/400°F for 1½ hours.

Remove the foil and cook for 20 minutes more, until the skin is crisp and brown. To check the chicken is completely cooked through, cut into the flesh between the leg and body; if the juices run clear, it is cooked.

Seasons for game birds

Pheasant
October 1st – January 31st. An old maxim is roast up to Christmas and put them in a casserole afterwards because they get tougher as the season goes on.

Grouse
August 12th – December 10th. Roast young birds and serve one per person. Casserole older birds.

Partridge
September 1st – January 31st. As for pheasant, roast up to Christmas and casserole after.

Roasting times for game birds

Pheasant

Oven temperature: Gas Mark 7/220°C/425°F.
Allow 20 minutes per 450 g (1 lb).

Partridge

Oven temperature: Gas Mark 6/200°C/400°F.
Allow 45 minutes total cooking.

Grouse

Oven temperature: Gas Mark 6/200°C/400°F.
Allow 35–45 minutes total cooking.

Gravy for roast chicken and meat

The secret ingredients are in the bottom of the roasting tin. Pour off any excess fat, add 1 tablespoon of flour, a stock cube (optional) and 1 teaspoon of marmite (optional). Using a wooden spoon or a balloon whisk, gradually add water (or the vegetable water) to the tin, over the heat, making sure all the bits are stirred in. Give it a good boil. Don't worry if it is lumpy, just pour through a sieve before serving.

Gravy embellishments

Add red or white wine, cider (great with pork),
a teaspoon of redcurrant jelly (good with lamb),
a splash of good vinegar or a teaspoon of
quince jelly (good with chicken and game).

*

" *The best sauce is cooked in an old pan* "

African proverb

To get crispy roast potatoes

Peel the potatoes, cut them into evenly sized pieces and boil in plenty of salted water for 10 minutes. Drain the potatoes in a colander and shake vigorously to 'ruffle' the outsides – this is what makes them crispy. Put 1 tablespoon of sunflower or olive oil into a shallow baking tray, add the potatoes and shake so they are covered with oil. Cook for 1 hour in a high oven (Gas mark 6/200°C/400°F) until crispy.

The Perfect Roast

"What I say is that, if a fellow really likes potatoes, he must be a pretty decent sort of fellow."

A A Milne, 1882–1956

"I heard the bells on Christmas Day;
their old familiar carols play,
and wild and sweet the word repeat
of peace on earth, good-will to men!"

Henry Wadsworth Longfellow, 1807–1882

Catering for Christmas

Choosing the turkey

Opt for a turkey no bigger than 9 kg (20 lb) –
the bigger the turkey the lesser the flavour;
5.4 kg–6.3 kg (12–14 lb) is the perfect size. Allow
1 kg (2 lb) per person as a good guide. Make a
note of the weight for calculating the cooking time.

If you have a large party, buy two smaller turkeys rather than one huge one.

＊

Allow at least two days to thaw a frozen turkey. You may be short of space in the fridge so find a safe place outside the warm house – the garage may come in handy. Make sure the turkey is in a dish or container large enough to catch drips, and keep it all well covered.

The stuffing

For a 5.4–6.3 kg (12–14 lb) turkey. Start with a packet mix and boiling water or whiz some fresh breadcrumbs in a food processor or blender. About 4–5 thick slices will do. Add 225 g (8 oz) sausage meat then any of the following:

Grated zest and juice of a lemon

✳

1 chopped onion or a couple of shallots,
fried in a knob of butter.

✳

Chopped fresh thyme, sage and/or parsley.

✳

Chopped peeled chestnuts – fresh, canned
or vacuum packed.

✳

Chopped dried apricots or chopped
dried cranberries.

✳

Add plenty of salt and freshly ground black pepper
and a couple of beaten eggs to moisten the
stuffing. Mix everything together with your hands.

Stuffing and preparing the turkey

Weigh the stuffing and make a note of it to calculate the cooking time. Stuff just before cooking. Remove the giblets from the turkey and keep for making gravy. Put the stuffing in the main cavity without packing it too tight. Pop a peeled and quartered onion into the other end, with a halved lemon if you like. Don't tie the legs together or truss the bird. Smother the breast and legs with softened butter using your hands. Then lay 4–5 rashers of rindless back bacon over the breast.

No need to stuff

Just pop half a lemon, a quartered onion (in its skin), a handful of parsley and a sprig of thyme into the cavity of the turkey before cooking.

Cooking the turkey

Add together the weight of turkey and stuffing.
Cook at Gas Mark 5/180°C/350°F for
20 minutes per 450 g (1lb), plus an extra
20 minutes. Fit the turkey snugly in a roasting
tin, pour in about 2.5 cm (1 in) water (this
helps keep the turkey moist and also gives a
good base for the gravy), then cover the whole
tray in foil. Remove the foil about 30 minutes
before the end of cooking to brown the turkey.

Is the turkey cooked?

To check that it is cooked, pierce the area
between the leg and the body of the turkey with
a sharp knife. The juices should run clear and
there should be no sign of blood. Transfer the
turkey to a warmed serving platter and cover
with foil. Let the turkey rest while you
make the gravy.

To make giblet stock

Boil the giblets for about 30 minutes in water
with 1 sliced onion, a sprig of thyme, some
parsley stalks, a bay leaf, salt and pepper.
Strain the stock for gravy.

Christmas pudding

Go for an upper-priced, good brand. Cook the pudding in the microwave if you can to save having another pan on the cooker. Not everyone likes Christmas pudding so offer a simple alternative such as fresh fruit salad and/or meringues.

*

"Love came down at Christmas; love all lovely, love divine; love was born at Christmas, stars and angels gave the sign."

Christina Rossetti, 1830–1894

Mince pies

There are also some excellent mince pies in the shops. Try lifting the lids and popping in a small blob of brandy butter. Then warm the pies for a few minutes in the oven (not in the microwave as it makes the pastry soggy). Sift over a little icing sugar before serving.

Mincemeat

If you buy the mincemeat for home-made pies,
add a couple of tablespoons of brandy or
whisky to each jar and stir well.

*The future... seems to me no unified
dream but a mince pie, long in the baking,
never quite done.*

Edward Young, 1683–1765

" *Cooking is like making love, you do it well, or you do not do it at all.* **"**

Harriet van Horne, b. 1920

" *I don't like gourmet cooking or 'this' cooking or 'that' cooking. I like good cooking.* **"**

James Beard, 1903–1985

Leftover Christmas pudding

If you love Christmas pudding, it is fantastic
the next day, sliced and fried in a little butter
until crispy on both sides and served with
brandy butter. (Try not to think of the calories.)

❝Eat what is cooked,
listen to what is said.❞

Russian proverb

"_Anyone who believes that men are the equal of women has never seen a man trying to wrap a Christmas present._**"**

Anon.

> **"** *If a pot is cooking, the friendship*
> *will stay warm.* **"**

Arab proverb